The Wharf, *c.*1895. This litho was published in Cassell's *Gazetteer of Great Britain and Ireland*, 1896. The original photograph was by Mr. Samuel Hawkes, of 3 High Street, Hungerford.

Tony & Stella
Thank you for your friendship over
the past 22 yrs! Keep well Love Brenda.

With Love and best wishes
John Julie and James

Many happy memories and love. Margie

Tony & Stella,

We hope you enjoy exploring
& sharing in your new community
Best wishes
Barbara & Chris.

Warmest wishes always - Rona & Neil.

Wishing you a Happy Retirement Mary.

Fondest memories of your friendship
to us in Wanborough
much love from Richard & Jane B.
xx

We've done some wonderful things
together - and still will. Thank you
both for everything. Good health
love Joyce & Hugh. xx

With much love and good wishes
from. Jane and Ian xxxxx

We're looking forward to your return visits!
With much love. Edna & David.

HUNGERFORD
A Pictorial History

Bridge Street, *c.*1914.

HUNGERFORD
A Pictorial History

Dr. Hugh Pihlens

Phillimore

1992

Published by
PHILLIMORE AND CO. LTD.
Shopwyke Hall, Chichester, Sussex

ISBN 0 85033 835 2

Printed and bound in Great Britain by
BIDDLES LTD.
Guildford, Surrey

To my wife Lois,
whose constant encouragement and help with historical research
have made such a major contribution towards
the preparation of this book

Town Hall,
Hungerford.

I delight in recommending to you this magnificent publication. I applaud the initiative of its publishers, and pay tribute to the untiring effort and enthusiasm of its compiler, Dr. Hugh Pihlens.

Since his arrival in the town some 19 years ago, Hugh's love of his subject has led him to publish in 1983 his own book, *The Story of Hungerford*, besides which he became the instigator of the Hungerford Historical Association, becoming its first Chairman, to be followed in this role later by his wife Lois. This flourishes today, in ever increasing importance and has become one of the town's most highly prized societies. During the intervening years the Pihlens have amassed a large collection of historical data on our town. It is not surprising, therefore, that Hugh should have been asked to compile this latest exciting volume. I endorse his remarks and gratitude to those other members of our community who have provided information and many photographs for inclusion, opening up their own prize collections and in many instances revealing, possibly for the first time, several unique views of this ancient town and inhabitants.

Hungerford is rightly proud of its heritage and traditions, which stretch back through the mists of time. For over six centuries this small town has jealously guarded its ancient rights and privileges, and largely conducted its own affairs. Its unique setting, within large areas of common land, in a beautiful corner of western Berkshire, is widely acknowledged. Its ancient High Street, and other picturesque corners of the town, are cherished by its inhabitants.

This marvellous collection of photographs will therefore find favour and a welcome spot upon the book-shelves of those who live within its bounds. I am confident also that it will portray to the casual visitor, the tourist and the historian, a very real picture of the town, its people, and its fabric of life over a period of many years – and give some clear indication to all of the great pleasure that is derived from being a Hungerfordian.

John L. Newton
Constable of Hungerford

List of Illustrations

Frontispiece: Bridge Street, *c.*1914

The King's Visit – 21-26 October 1912

Illustration Acknowledgements

I wish to thank the following people for allowing me to borrow their photographs and postcards, and for giving me permission to reproduce them in this book. Old photographs are often prized possessions and, without the generosity of the many owners, this book would not have been possible. Within the limits of one book, it is not possible to cover every aspect of the town's history. I trust, however, that readers will find that the final choice does include an interesting and wide variety of subjects.

In addition to the people listed below, there are many others who have kindly loaned photographs which could not be selected because of pressure of space. To them, and everyone who has helped in the production of the book, I extend my sincere thanks:

Mr. John Allen, 156; Mrs. Janet Cleverley, 72, 74-76, 78, 90; Mrs. Marjorie Eatwell, 9, 18, 79, 86, 103, 104, 109, 112, 149; Mrs. Beatrice Goodman, 129; Mr. Stewart Hofgartner, 3, 27-29, 58, 130, 136, 143, 155; Mrs. Barbara Hope, 8, 20, 37, 65, 113, 115, 162; Dr. Humphrey Hope, 10, 68, 80, 158, 159, 163-66, 168, 170; Mrs. Sue Hopson, endpapers, 34, 35, 93, 100, 107, 128, 150, 160; Mrs. Freda Horwood, 97, 134; Col. Donald Macey, 22, 41, 47-49, 51, 52, 89, 101, 102, 106, 131, 132, 135, 140; Miss Betty Munford, 21, 61, 83, 92, 116, 125, 147; Mr. John Newton, 57, 88, 117-21, 139; Mrs. Rosemary Oldfield, 12, 16, 38, 63, 108; Mr. Darren Prestoe, 19; Hungerford Primary School, 146, 148; Miss Ann Rivers, 32, 39, 56, 77, 87, 91, 96, 98, 127, 154; Mr. Ron Scott, 17, 31, 33, 42, 145; Mrs. Doris Taylor, 26, 60, 81, 82, 84; Mrs. Val Troke, 137; Mr. Robin Tubb and family, 13, 14, 30, 36, 53, 54, 62, 122, 123, 141, 144, 167; Mr. George Willett, 25, 66, 94.

Pictures supplied by the author: 1, 2, 4, 5, 7, 11, 15, 23, 24, 40, 43-46, 50, 55, 59, 64, 67, 69-71, 73, 95, 99, 105, 110, 111, 114, 124, 126, 133, 138, 142, 151-53, 157, 161, 169.

My thanks are also due to the many people who have contributed background information for the book. The owners of the photographic originals listed above have in many cases provided historical comments on their photographs, but other contributors include Mr. Paul Lacey (re G.W.R. bus service); Mrs. Ruth Lewington (re Mr. Albert Parsons); the National Motor Museum, Beaulieu (re Mr. Parsons' car); the Shuttleworth Collection (re the Bristol Prier aeroplane).

Introduction

The attractive rural market town of Hungerford is at the very western end of Berkshire, near the borders with Wiltshire and Hampshire. It lies in the North Wessex Downs Area of Outstanding Natural Beauty. A walk around the town and its immediate surrounding countryside will reveal the inherent charm of the area. Much of the town has remained unaltered for generations.

Archaeological excavations on the northern outskirts of Hungerford in 1989 revealed stone age tools and the site of a bronze age ceremonial building. A Roman road passes just north of the town on its way from Silchester and Speen in the east through Littlecote estate to Mildenhall and Bath in the west. This early information begins the jigsaw of local history, but little of real detail can possibly be known about the town until written records begin.

The Domesday Survey, carried out by King William I in 1086, does not name Hungerford, although many of the manors immediately adjacent to the town are recorded, including Eddington, Leverton, Inkpen, Denford, Avington, Inglewood and Charlton. For the first written evidence of the town, one has to wait just a few years more until 1108, when documents refer to the church of Hungerford being assigned to the Abbey of Bec-Hellouin in Normandy. Of this church there are no remains, although there is a beautiful Norman church standing today in an idyllic setting at Avington, just a mile or so east of Hungerford.

The present parish church of St Lawrence was built in 1816, and stands on the site of an Early English predecessor. It is probable that, in turn, this church had been built on the site of the earlier Norman building. The church lies several hundred metres to the west of the town centre. In Norman times it is likely that the village was clustered around the church, on land now known as The Croft, and spreading on to Freemen's Marsh.

Around the end of the 12th century, a new town plan was conceived. This consisted of a main street running roughly north-south, with back lanes on either side of the main street, about a hundred metres to the east and west. The area contained within this framework was divided into narrow burgage plots, and within these the new town of Hungerford was built. The overall structure is still visible today, although sadly only a few of the High Street properties retain their long gardens reaching back to Prospect Road in the west, and Fairview Road in the east.

Through the 11th to 14th centuries the manor of Hungerford passed between the Crown and various Duchies of Leicester and Lancaster. In 1351 it was in the ownership of Henry, Duke of Lancaster, who married Isabel of Beaumont. Henry died in 1361 leaving no sons, but two daughters, Maud and Blanche. Maud inherited the estates, but died childless on 10 April 1362; and the manor of Hungerford, along with many other estates, passed to her younger sister, Blanche, wife of Edward III's fourth son, John of Gaunt. This date is therefore of some interest to Hungerfordians.

The connection with John of Gaunt is remembered today in the naming of some important buildings, such as the *John of Gaunt Inn* and John o'Gaunt Comprehensive School, and also streets, including Lancaster Square and Lancaster Close.

Chief of the traditions surrounding Hungerford's association with John of Gaunt is that he granted the right of fishing on the River Kennet from Eldren Stubb (just below Leverton in the west) as far as Irish Stile (at least two miles below Kintbury in the east). To support this tradition there is in the town's possession an ancient (and battered!) brass horn, which is said to have been given to the town by John of Gaunt as guarantee of those rights. There was a written charter confirming these rights, but the Duchy copy was lost in a fire at John of Gaunt's Savoy Palace in The Strand in 1381, and the town's copy was allegedly stolen in the days of Queen Elizabeth I. The loss of the charter occurred when there was increasing hostility between the Duchy and the townspeople over various rights and privileges. Many legal wrangles ensued, and at one stage the town appealed to the Queen herself in an attempt to win the day.

In the reign of James I, the long-standing legal disputes were settled, and in 1612 the King granted the Manor of Hungerford to two local men, John Eldred and William Whitmore. After a further few years of legal transfers, the Manor of Hungerford was conveyed in 1617 to Ralph Mackerell (Constable), and 13 other local men 'in trust for the inhabitants'. These 14 men thus became the first feoffees or trustees of the Town and Manor of Hungerford. The present commoners are those people owning and living in the properties established at the time of the 1612 James I grant.

The organisation of the Town and Manor of Hungerford has been handed down from generation to generation for nearly 400 years. The Commoners' Court is headed by the Constable, who is ably supported by a group of other officials including the Port-Reeve, Bailiff, four Tutti-men, a number of Water-Bailiffs, several Overseers of the Common (Port Down), three Keepers of the Keys of the Common Coffer, two Ale-Tasters (or 'Testers'), and the Bellman and Assistant Bailiff. Some offices have fallen from usage, including the Searchers and Sealers of Leather, and the Tasters of Flesh and Fish!

The most important day in the life of the Town and Manor is Tutti-Day, always held on the second Tuesday after Easter. In the past this was the day by which all quit rents and fines were due to be paid, and it marks the end of the financial and administrative year. The Bellman (who is also Town Crier) summons all the Commoners to the Commoners' Court, which is held in the Town Hall at 9 o'clock. Meanwhile the two Tutti-men, accompanied by their guide and mentor, the Orangeman, work their way around the town, visiting every house with common rights, numbering nearly 100 in total. In the past they would have collected the 'head penny' from each householder, but nowadays the most they collect is a kiss from the ladies of the house, and a little hospitality to help them on their way.

Meanwhile, in the Town Hall, the Commoners' Court is under way. The Constable guides the Court through a series of stages which are carried out today much as they have been for generations. The officers are elected for the coming year, the accounts are read and agreed, and a number of other matters are discussed concerning the affairs of the Town and Manor.

In 1908 the Town and Manor became a registered charity, and is thus responsible to the Charity Commissioners. The present trustees and court have a considerable responsibility, managing the Town Hall (probably the only Town Hall in the country not paid for by the Community Charge), the *John of Gaunt Inn*, the Common, Freemen's Marsh, as well as the extensive fishing in the Rivers Kennet and Dun.

In 1688 a very important part of British history took place in Hungerford. The Catholic King James II was King of England, but he was not widely popular, and by 1688 there were plans to remove him from the throne. The Protestant Prince William of Orange landed at Brixham in Devon, and travelled with his army towards London, hoping to gather support for his cause along the way. When the King learned of this approach, James II sent three commissioners to meet Prince William. The meeting took place in the *Bear Inn* at Hungerford on 6 December 1688, and it was during this meeting that plans were made for the throne of England to pass to William. The very fact that such a crucial meeting took place in Hungerford is evidence, if any were necessary, of the importance of the London to Bath Road, one of the major routes of the country. The fact that Hungerford lay on the Bath Road had a considerable effect on the town's growth and development. Coaching became big business, and Hungerford became a coaching town.

As early as 1228 there are written records of an important road through Savernake Forest from the east. This 'King's Way' was the forerunner of the Bath Road, and it crossed the River Kennet at the 'pons de Hungreford', recorded in 1275. Savernake Forest was much larger then, and surveys of the forest describe it as extending as far as 'the house of lepers at Hungerford'. In 1232 the Priory of St John was established on land at the northern edge of the town, now the site of Bridge Street. The priory was dissolved by Henry VIII in 1548.

During the Elizabethan period road travel began to be used more widely; one of the Queen's coachmen is known to have been buried in the parish churchyard in 1601. By 1740 traffic along the Bath Road had increased greatly, and at this time the access to the town from the Bath Road was improved. The ford through the River Dun (adjacent to the present war memorial) was proving very inadequate, and land was bought in order to build a new road with bridges – now the northern end of Bridge Street.

Hungerford lay not only on the Bath Road (running east-west) but also on the Oxford to Salisbury turnpike (running north-south). During the hey-day of the coaching period, at the end of the 18th century and the first few decades of the 19th century, the town grew and prospered. There were many coaching inns around the town servicing the coaching trade, along with many stables and blacksmiths. A new Town Hall was built in 1786, and many of the timber-framed High Street properties were 'modernised' by the addition of new Georgian frontages.

The prosperity of the town was further enhanced by the opening of the Kennet and Avon Canal in 1810. Hungerford wharf was a busy trading centre, and brought valuable business to the town. Census figures show that the population rose from 1987 in the year 1,801 to 2,696 in 1851, a very considerable growth of 35 per cent. There seems little doubt that this first half of the 19th century was Hungerford's busiest, but the opening of Brunel's Great Western Railway to Bristol in 1841 spelt disaster to the canal trade. Journeys that had taken more than a week by canal could now be accomplished in just a few hours. Both the canal trade and coaching traffic slumped.

It seemed that only one thing could help Hungerford – the building of a railway to the town. This came sooner than many would have dreamed of, and a terminus station was opened (on the site of the present station) in 1847. This line was later extended (in 1862) onwards to the west, and one could have expected that Hungerford would continue to thrive, now that it lay on a main railway route. The expected prosperity failed to materialise, however. Rather than bringing trade to the town, the railway drained the town of people and resources. The population actually fell between 1851 and 1901.

Despite the many problems at the time, Hungerford's civic pride ran high. A new Town Hall and Corn Exchange were built, and several new churches. Two important iron foundries provided employment for many men in the town, and with the continuing role of market town for the local area, Hungerford reached the 20th century as a busy and active community. The Hungerford Water Works was established in 1903, and mains drainage in 1909. Telephones were installed in 1907, a splendid new all-age Council School was built in 1910, and a new post office in 1914. Many of the photographs in this book date from the early 20th century, and the atmosphere of the town can be assessed through them.

The outbreak of the First World War had a profound effect on the town. Many men went to fight, whilst the town itself was host to an army unit assembling here before joining the front.

The years after the First World War saw the town begin its great 20th-century expansion. Until that time there had been very few houses outside the main streets of High Street, Bridge Street, Cow Lane (Park Street) and Church Street. Post-war, however, there was an accelerating expansion. This was a time of great community spirit, with a strong emphasis locally on sports and games. A sports ground in The Croft was opened in 1921, and bowls, croquet, tennis, shooting, rugby, football and cricket all thrived. There was even a golf course on the Common.

More recently the town has grown more, and the building of the M4 motorway in 1971 has brought further prosperity to the whole Kennet Valley. Modern Hungerford is well known for its antique shops, and as a tourist centre. The Kennet and Avon Canal was restored at Hungerford in 1974, and fully reopened in August 1990. It provides enjoyment for many, whether in boats or on the tow-path.

With only a few exceptions, the photographs in this book are dated between 1850 and 1930; most date from 1900 to 1920. We are fortunate to have had some excellent photographers in Hungerford and the surrounding area. Foremost of these was Albert Parsons, who came to Hungerford in 1902, and worked here until his death in 1950. The high quality of his work and the large range of photographs he took provide us with a splendid record of the period. Mention should also be made of William Softley Parry, a toy dealer and photographer in Bridge Street in the 1870s. Two of a fine set of early Cartes de Visite dated c.1875 showing views around Hungerford are used in this book. Other Hungerford photographers include William Mapson of Church Street and High Street, and Samuel Hawkes of High Street.

In 1907 the Reading photographer P. O. Collier began his photographic record of Berkshire, and several examples are included. Other visiting photographers making important contributions to the Hungerford photographic records include Francis Frith, Benjamin Stone, whose large series of photographs dated 1902 exists, and Charles Hawker of Newbury. During the First World War, the firm of J. Templeman of Stoke-on-Trent took the official photographs of the army unit here, but at the same time took some other local views.

Among them all, their photographs provide a very complete record of life in the town at that time. The results these early photographers achieved were all the more remarkable when one considers the equipment and materials they were using. As we enjoy the fruits of their handiwork, we must be grateful for their care and artistic skills, and thankful also to the many people who have kept or collected local photographs over the years.

Sources and Bibliography

Directories:
Universal British, 1792
Berkshire, 1796
Pigot & Co., 1823 and later
Kelly, 1847 and later
Billing, 1854 and later
Post Office, 1869 and later
Cosburn, 1883 and later

Census data, 1801 and later
Commoner's Lists, 1781 and later

Cannon, P., *A Directory of Photographers*, Newbury & District 1854-1945 (1991)
Historical Record of 180 Company R.A.S.C. (1920)
Lewis, Peter, *Squadron Histories 1912-59* (1959)
Norris, Geoffrey, *The Royal Flying Corps – A History* (1965)
Pihlens, Dr. H. L., *A Walk About Hungerford* (1988)
Pihlens, Dr. H. L., *The Story of Hungerford* (1983)
Summers, The Rev. W. H., *The Story of Hungerford in Berkshire* (1926)

List of Photographers and Publishers, with Dates of Local Plates

Ernest Barnard, Hungerford, 1906-18 – 26, 66, 74, 89, 98.
Alfred Barratt, Fleet Street, London, 1911 – 51.
Chester Vaughan, 1903 – 8, 25.
P. O. Collier, Reading, 1905-40 – 41, 68, 87, 107, 114, 128, 133, 136, 154.
Elliott and Fry, London, 1910 – 152.
Freeman's lithographic series, 1903 – 3, 27-29, 94.
Freeman's photographic series, 1910 – 9.
Charles Hawker, Newbury, 1883-1937 – 143, 155.
Samuel Hawkes, Hungerford, 1887-1909 – endpapers.
A. W. Hoare, Reading, 1930 – 52.
Frederick Jessett, Eddington, 1907-8 – 109, 113.
William Mapson, Hungerford and Pewsey, 1898-1905 – 60, 135.
William Softley Parry, Bridge Street, Hungerford, 1876-83 – 57, 139
Albert Parsons, Hungerford, 1902-50 – 10, 12, 14-21, 23, 30, 31, 33-39, 43-50, 53-56,
    59, 63, 69-71, 74-79, 84-86, 92, 93, 96, 100, 108, 112, 115, 122-27, 129, 131, 140,
    141, 146, 147, 151, 156-170.
J. Benjamin Stone, 1902 – 144.
J. Templeman, Stoke-on-Trent, 1914-1918 – 61, 81, 82.
W. Wicks, Hayes, Middlesex, 1910 – 153.
Wyndham Series, c.1904 – 32, 40.

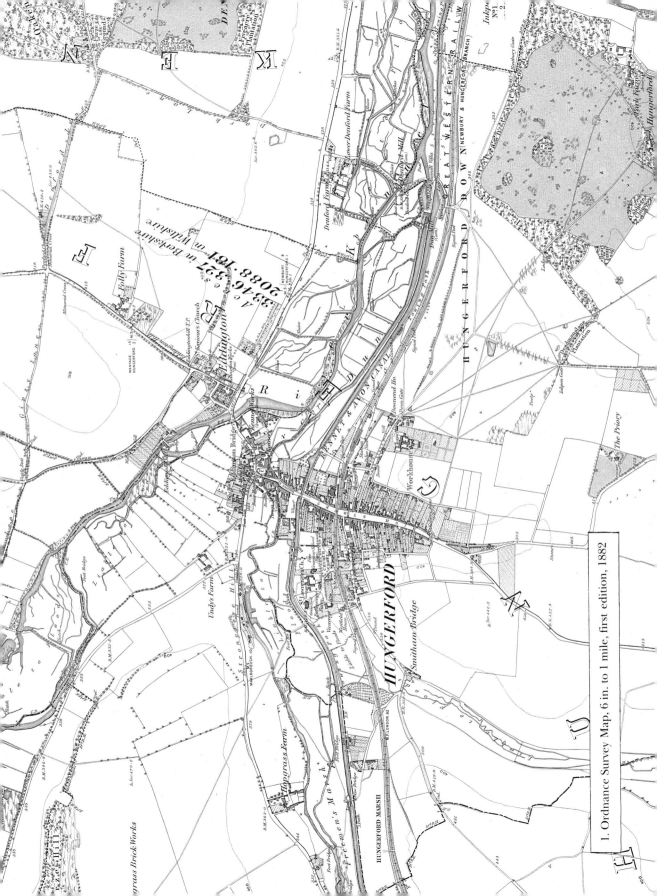

1. Ordnance Survey Map, 6 in. to 1 mile, first edition, 1882

The Bear Hotel

2. The Bear Corner, *c.*1910. This scene is familiar to everyone who has travelled the Bath Road. On the right is the *Bear Hotel*, a coaching inn whose origins date back to the 13th century. There are written records surviving from 1464. It was here that the commissioners of King James I met Prince William of Orange in 1688 before he claimed the Crown of England. Riverside House (now Riverside Antiques) stands proudly overlooking the scene, whilst on the left are Charlie Batchelor's furniture shop, and Jessett's bakery (now private houses).

The Town Halls and the Market Place

3. The Town Hall, *c.*1902. Hungerford's Town Hall and Corn Exchange is an imposing building dominating the Market Place. Posters on the railings outside advertise film shows which were regularly held in the Corn Exchange until the Regal Cinema (demolished 1974) opened at the top of 'Picture Hill' (now Atherton Hill). On the left is the Crown Brewery, run by Elisha Love, shown here just before the addition of a mock-Tudor frontage.

4. Ye Olde Town Hall, 1862. Hungerford has had at least four town halls. The first, perhaps dating back to the time of John of Gaunt in the 14th century, was recorded in a survey by the Duchy of Lancaster of 1543/4 as being 'ruinous and utterly dekeyed'. In 1607 a new town hall was built, which was to last until the late 1700s. This early glass plate shows the third town hall, built 1786, standing in the middle of the market-place, and surmounted by its octagonal cupola. Spanning the High Street beyond the Town Hall is Hungerford's original railway bridge, built in 1862 to carry the railway further west. This bridge was later replaced in 1896 by the lattice bridge seen in several other photographs in this book.

5. The Town Hall and Market Place, June 1862. Mr. Hall, the Magistrate's Clerk, gave to the town a grand four-face clock. To accommodate it, a new clock-tower was built on the Town Hall in 1862 replacing the earlier (and better proportioned) cupola, seen in the previous photograph. Opposite the Town Hall can be seen (from left to right) the *Three Swans Inn* (now *Three Swans Hotel*), the *Bell Inn* (now *Emma Jane* boutique), and Edwin Wiggins, blacksmith (later Charles Oakes, and now Hampton's estate agents). To the right of Cow Lane (now Park Street) is the *Plume of Feathers Inn* (now the *Plume Inn*), and Bodman's drapery store (until recently Richard Astor's art gallery).

6. The two Town Halls, 1871. For a few months only there were two Town Halls in Hungerford. In the foreground is the 1786 building. Its clock-tower is empty, the clock having been transferred to the tower of the newly-built Corn Exchange and Town Hall behind. Between January and April 1872 the old building was demolished, some of the materials being used to build cottages in Church Street.

The Church, The Croft and the Old Town Layout

7. Print of Hungerford church, *c.*1813. The parish church of Hungerford stands, somewhat unusually, well away from the centre of the town. It was first mentioned in a document dated 1108, and that original building was replaced by one in the Early English style during the 13th century. By the early 1800s this building had become so dilapidated that it was in danger of falling down. In 1811 major repairs were undertaken, but as soon as the work was completed, part of the original building collapsed bringing with it the newly-completed tower. This print shows the crumbling church and tower, its bell now removed to a wooden gantry under the trees on the left.

8. The parish church and the canal, 1903. When the Early English church collapsed, there was clearly no alternative but to build a completely new church. In 1814 an Act of Parliament was obtained, authorising the vicar, churchwardens and trustees to raise £6,000 for the task. In the end the new church was to cost £30,000, the balance being raised partly by private donations, and partly by a tontine, a form of cumulative insurance rarely heard of nowadays. The remaining portion of the old church was demolished, and in its place a new Georgian Gothic building was erected, designed by Mr. Pinch of Bath, and consecrated on 30 August 1816. Standing so close to the canal which had opened just a few years earlier in 1810, it is not surprising that it was built in Bath stone.

9. The church gate, *c.*1910. To celebrate the completion of the restoration, a set of new gates was installed at the churchyard entrance. These double gates, with adjacent kissing gate, were donated by the Town and Manor of Hungerford in 1886. The gas lamps seen in this photograph were replaced in 1940 by an electric light on an arch over the gateway, a gift of Mr. and Mrs. Astley.

10. The vicarage, *c.*1920. Standing adjacent to the churchyard is the vicarage, dating from the 17th century. In this photograph you can see clear evidence of that popular sport of the clergy – a croquet hoop! The vicarage stands very close to the canal, and in order to keep his three young children safe when playing in the garden, the vicar (the Rev. Tom Gray, see plate 123) sometimes tethered them to trees. One bishop commented after visiting the vicar: 'Hungerford is the only place I know where the children are tied up, and the dogs are loose'!

11. The Church Croft, *c.*1895. The Croft is a quiet green away from the hustle and bustle of the High Street. It is said that the Church Croft was given to the town by John Undewes and his wife for 'a place to sport therein' at the nominal rent of a red rose yearly if demanded. Such a rent is not demanded, and The Croft is now part of the Town and Manor land. It was in this area surrounding the church that the original village of Hungerford probably stood, until the new town plan was laid out at the end of the 12th century. On the left is a tiled building clearly recognisable as the present day Hungerford Club House. The thatched cottages beyond have been demolished, but the tiled and gabled cottage in the distance still stands (1 The Croft).

12. Church Croft Avenue, *c.*1911. The straight roadway running along the northern edge of The Croft, joining Little Church Lane (now Church Lane) and the church, was known as Croft Avenue. The avenue was lined by some very tall trees, possibly elms or large-leafed limes. They had been planted *c.*1840 to replace an earlier avenue of elms. The children help to show how tall the trees had become.

13. The Croft, *c.*1890. One's eye is immediately drawn to the children in this photograph, standing carefully positioned for best effect. Perhaps the most special feature of this early print, however, is that it is one of the rare photographs showing the old Free Grammar School, established by the Rector of Welford, the Rev. Thomas Sheaffe in 1635. It is the building to the right of the trees in line with the church tower. The Grammar School existed until 1884 and the building was eventually demolished to make way for the Church House in 1900 (see plate 16).

14. Sweet chestnuts in The Croft, 1912. The trees shown in plates 12 and 13 eventually became too tall and needed replacement. In 1912 an avenue of young sweet chestnuts was planted. On the left, in the bowler hat, is Mr. Henry d'Oyley Wolvey Astley, who was a local solicitor and Clerk to the Town and Manor. With the still relatively slow shutter speeds available on an overcast day, the identity of the other man planting this tree must remain a mystery!

15. The Croft, c.1913. With the felling of the old trees, The Croft assumed a fresh and less oppressive air. The old tracks across The Croft can clearly be seen, with St Lawrence's church and the Church House in the background.

16. Church House, c.1911. After the Grammar School had closed in 1884 (see plate 13), the site was sold in November 1898 to Sir William George Pearce (of Chilton Lodge, see plate 27), who built the Church House (now Croft Hall) in 1900. Sir William Pearce gave the premises to the town, along with an endowment in his will. Church House was used as a library, for the Sunday School, and by the Church House Club (formed in 1901) before the bowling green, croquet lawn and tennis courts were developed in 1921.

17. Church House sports section, 1923. The sports ground was laid out on land between The Croft and the canal. The plan was different from the modern layout, and two tennis courts can be seen on the site of the present-day bowling green. The three tall poplar trees are adjacent to Hungerford canal lock.

Sports Clubs

18. Married v. Single football, 1921. The 1920s were years when sport featured strongly in the life of Hungerford. Teams and matches were arranged with almost every combination imaginable. This photograph shows the teams taking part in the annual Football Club match between the married and single men.

19. Hungerford Swifts Football Club, 1908-9. The football club at this time was at the western edge of the town, beyond Smitham Bridge, near The Orchard in Marsh Lane.

20. Ladies v. Gents cricket, 1913. The cricket club, under the captaincy of the Rev. John Denning (see plate 23), played many local elevens. In August each year there was always good support for the Ladies v. Gents match, when the men played with a bat more suitable to rounders than cricket!

21. Lancastrian Tennis Club, 1914. Before the tennis courts were made in The Croft, tennis was played at the Lancastrian Tennis Club, on what is now the Primary School field, off Fairview Road. In the background you can see the Council School building, opened in 1910 (see plate 146).

22. Astor Challenge Rifle Cup, 21 June 1906. The Hungerford and District Rifle Club won the Astor Challenge Cup (Berkshire County) in 1906. The team comprised: W. Blake (Capt.), 84; E. Clements, 83; W. Chapman, 82; A. Bartholomew, 77; A. Macklin, 78; and P. Jessett, 72; Total, 476. The result was a tight one, with the other teams scoring as follows: Wokingham, 475; Windsor, 440; Reading, 428; Newbury Guildhall, 427; and Bucklebury, 209. Poor Bucklebury – not a good day!

23. The Rev. John F. C. Denning, M.A., c.1921. In addition to being curate of Hungerford from 1889 to 1895, Mr. Denning was headmaster of Westfield House School in Parsonage Lane from 1893 until it closed c.1906. Westfield House was a Boys' Day and Boarding Classical and Mathematical School established in 1842 (now a private house). Even when he was no longer curate, Denning continued to help in the parish, and is remembered for holding regular morning services at the Workhouse, afternoon services at Hungerford Newtown, and also managing to fit in services at the chapel at Denford Park, using a rather old-fashioned bicycle as his means of transport. He was a keen sportsman, and especially good at cricket, as were his brother and two sons. This photograph shows him with his splendid collection of sporting trophies.

The Great Estates around the Town

24. Hungerford Park House, c.1920. Hungerford is surrounded by a small number of large country estates. The land to the east and south belonged to Hungerford Park House, built c.1795 in the Italian style. This photograph shows the Garden Front, with its croquet lawn and two tennis courts. An earlier house, built by Queen Elizabeth I for her favourite, Robert Devereux, Earl of Essex, stood on this site, and had been the home of the Barons of Hungerford. The house shown in this photograph was demolished in 1960 and only the imposing gates and lodges remind us of its former glory. The estate is now owned by Lord Howard de Walden, of Avington Manor.

25. Littlecote House, c.1920. To the west of Hungerford is land belonging to Littlecote House. This splendid Tudor manor house contains a fine collection of Cromwellian armour, and in the grounds there are remains of an important group of Roman buildings including an Orpheus mosaic.

26. Chilton Lodge, 1918. To the north of the town is the estate of Chilton Lodge, now owned by Mr. Gerald Ward. For about seven hundred years this was the seat of the Whitelocke family, one of whom, Bulstrode Whitelocke, a distinguished character of the Civil War and Commonwealth period, died there in 1676. The estate was afterwards sold to John Holwell, one of the sufferers in the 'Black Hole' of Calcutta, and subsequently governor. At the beginning of the 19th century the property belonged to John Pearse M.P., who demolished the old mansion and built another. This was enlarged, and almost entirely reconstructed c.1890, by Sir William George Pearce, who created a fine Georgian style stone building, with a handsome portico supported on Corinthian columns. The kitchen gardens have been made famous by the past head gardener, Mr. Harry Dodson, whose television series on the Victorian kitchen garden was broadcast in 1987.

27. Eddington House, 1903. Standing about one mile north of the village of Eddington, Eddington House owned land to the north and east of Hungerford. The house is in two distinct parts, that to the left (south) is rendered with a stucco cornice and parapet, and dates from the early 1800s, whilst the northern part is a late 19th-century addition in red brick. During the early 1900s it was owned by Major E. R. Portal, one of whose five sons was to become Chief of the Air Staff during the Second World War. Air Chief Marshal Sir Charles Portal, K.C.B., C.B., D.S.O., M.C., was known locally as 'Peter', and was a keen member of the local cricket club, as were his father and brothers.

28. Inglewood House, 1903. Inglewood lies between Hungerford and Kintbury. It was one of the great houses of the Knights Templar during the Crusade of 1108, and became a Royal Falconry in the reign of Henry VIII. The fine mansion shown in this photograph was built *c.*1820, and was sold by the owner Colonel Walmesley in 1929 for use as a Catholic college by the De La Salle brothers. It is currently a well-known health hydro.

29. Denford House, 1903. The manor of Denford dates from before Domesday, but the house in this photograph was built in 1832 and was designed by Sir Jeffry Wyatville. The owner, George Henry Cherry, was Sheriff of Berkshire in 1829. The house and manor later passed to his sons, George Charles Cherry (who was Sheriff of Berkshire in 1871), and Major-General Apsley Cherry. On the latter's death in 1907, the estate passed to his own son Apsley Cherry-Garrard, who served under Captain Scott in his famous Antarctic expedition.

30 and 31. The Hungerford Town Brass and Reed Band, 1912. These two photographs show the Town Band at Denford Park on the occasion of their first concert with new instruments. The then owner of the house, Captain Sawbridge (standing in the formal group in the back row, just to the left of centre), had loaned the finance to purchase the instruments, music and music pouches. In 1953 Denford Park became a junior school for New Hall, Chelmsford, run by the Canonesses of the Holy Sepulchre, until Norland Nursery Training College (founded in 1892) bought it in 1967. It is now the Norland College.

32. Freemen's Marsh, 1904. The town is contained on the west by ancient common lands known as Freemen's Marsh, through which runs the River Dun. This enchanting photograph shows a tranquil scene of river and marsh, with the thatched cottages at Strongrove Hill in the distance. Occasionally when studying old postcards, one comes across a gem! The message on one copy of this card includes the text, 'Do you recognise Auntie Amy on this card? She was taken when out sketching'.

33. Marsh View Cottages, *c.*1920. At the end of Marsh Lane, the road leading onto Freemen's Marsh, there was a terrace of cottages running up the slope from the road. These cottages, Marsh View, were demolished in the mid-1970s, and a group of new houses has been built on the site.

34. The Common Port Down, *c.*1910. On the high ground to the east of the town is the Common – an unspoilt area of 202 acres used over the years for a wide variety of recreational purposes, including golf and steam fairs! The Common is owned and managed by the Town and Manor of Hungerford, and the Commoners have rights of grazing cattle on the land.

35. Down Gate, *c.*1910. The main entrance to the Common is at the Down Gate, where there is a small group of cottages with enviable views across the open ground. Adjacent to the gate is a pub called the *Down Gate*, previously known as *The Royal Exchange*, and during the 19th century as the *Spotted Cow*.

36. *(left)* Aeroplane on the Common, 1912. There are many photographs of early aeroplanes which landed on the Common; they caused great local interest, and the local photographer, Albert Parsons, was clearly very interested. He later joined the Royal Flying Corps. This one is very close to the Down Gate. It is a Bristol Prier two-seater monoplane, one of which was used by No. 3 Squadron, R.F.C. in 1912, until grounded by the law on the use of monoplanes in September that year.

37. *(below left)* Eddington from the Common, *c*.1920. This view from the western edge of the Common looks across the railway goods yard and the Kennet valley towards Eddington village. St Saviour's church can be seen on the rising ground at the extreme right of the photograph.

38. *(below)* Dun Mill, *c*.1910. With so much water around the town, it is not surprising that there are many water-mills. Indeed, several mills were mentioned in the Domesday Book of 1086, and there are written records of Dun Mill since 1494. Despite its name, Dun Mill lies on the River Kennet. It was a fulling mill during the 17th century, and the present mill dates from the 18th century. When the canal was built immediately adjacent to it, the owners were able to take great advantage of an alternative means of transport to and from the mill. There has been a famous trout farm here since 1907.

THE BERKSHIRE TROUT FARM
HUNGERFORD.

39. Dun Mill Bridge and Denford Mill, *c*.1920. The water in the immediate foreground is the Kennet and Avon Canal, and beyond this is one branch of the River Kennet, with its charming triple-arched bridge downstream from Dun Mill. In the background is Denford Mill, a five-bay working mill with the miller's house on its right.

40. Denford Mill, 1904. The mill was used during the 19th century as a fulling mill in the cloth industry, for which a copious supply of water was required. In this photograph it can be seen that the mill is still working, many years before being converted for residential use.

41. Eddington Mill, *c.*1911. The manor of Eddington is listed in Domesday with a mill and over 500 acres. The 1844 edition of *The Miller* states that Eddington Mill flour was well known throughout the West Country. The mill continued to mill flour until *c.*1952, after which it was used for fertiliser storage until finally closing in 1959.

42. Digging Eddington Lake, 1922. Upstream of Eddington Mill is a fine lake. This photograph shows the work in progress, with Eddington Mill at the far end of the excavations, on the left.

Beating the Bounds

43. Beating The Bounds, 8 July 1913. Tradition has it that each year the elders of all towns should walk around the town limits, ensuring that the boundary is secure and undisputed. This excursion should involve as many members of the community as possible, both young and old, so that everyone shall come to know the boundary markers, and future generations shall be able to protect the boundary. In 1913 the local photographer, Albert Parsons, followed the Beating of the Bounds, and his very complete photographic record, of which a small selection is included here, provides us with a wonderful insight into a particular day in the life of Hungerford. At various points they stop to consult the map, to ensure that the exact boundary is followed.

44. The party takes a rest during the long excursion. This photograph was probably taken at Denford Mill, looking north towards Lower Denford cottages, with Mill Cottage on the right of the photograph.

BEATING THE BOUNDS HUNGERFORD 8.7.13

718

"BUMPING"

45. Bumping. In order to make the exact position of the many boundary posts more memorable to the party, it was customary for one or other of the younger members of the group to be upended at each post, and to have his head (gently) 'bumped' on it. Few youngsters would fail to remember the experience vividly, and they would be able to pass on their local knowledge to future generations.

46. Wading through the river. Many of Hungerford's boundaries lie along one or other of the local rivers, and in order to Beat the Bounds properly, there is no alternative to wading in and struggling onward through waist-high water. It should be noted that this particular expedition took place in July, when the walk through the river would not have been too unpleasant!

Town and Manor — Tutti-Day

47. Constable, Bellman, and Tutti-men, Hocktide 1910. The Constable, Mr. Alfred Allright (grocer) is seated, holding the Lucas Horn, dating from 1634. Behind him is the Bellman, Mr. Edward Bushnell, and on either side are the two Tutti-men, Mr. Frederick Macklin (of the dairy, left) and Mr. Robert Cole (of the Town Mill, right), holding their Tutti-poles. It is thought that the Tutti-poles derive from the west country name for a nose-gay, or bunch of sweet-smelling flowers. No doubt the Tutti-men were glad of their tutties when visiting some of the less sweet-smelling parts of the town in times gone by!

48. Collecting the Commoner's Penny, Hocktide
1914. On the morning of Tutti-Day, the Assistant
Bailiff, who is also the Bellman and Town Crier,
walks the length of the High Street and Bridge
Street, summoning all Commoners to the Hocktide
Court. Any Commoner who is unable to attend is
liable to be fined one penny, lest he forfeit his
rights to grazing and fishing for the year.

49. 'At 9 o'clock in the forenoon', Hocktide 1910.
The Constable (Mr. Alfred Allright) is about to
send the Tutti-men (Mr. Alfred Macklin on the left,
and Mr. Robert Cole on the right) to visit all the
Commoners' houses in the town. Some of the
Commoners can be seen behind him, waiting to
attend the Hocktide Court, which starts at nine
o'clock.

   Both plates 47 and 49 date from Hocktide 1910,
and it is interesting to note that plate 47 shows
Frederick Macklin as Tutti-man, whilst plate 49
shows his son Alfred. This is the only known
occasion when father and son shared the duty of
Tutti-man on the same day!

50. The Hocktide Court, 1913. The court sits in the Town Hall, and is chaired by the constable (Mr. John Adnams, corn and seed merchant), with members of the jury and other Commoners around the table. Seated (from left to right) are Messrs. F. Macklin (dairyman), G. Winterbourne (florist), T. W. Alexander (grocer), G. Wren (saddler and ironmonger), ?, Dr. H. P. Major (doctor), J. Adnams (constable), H. d'O. W. Astley (solicitor), W. Mapson (watchmaker), ?, and I. Beard (coal merchant). Standing (from left to right) are Messrs. W. H. Belcher, E. S. Gingell (grocer), E. W. Batt (baker), H. Crossley (Tutti-man), E. Bushnell (Bellman), J. S. Tyler (draper, Tutti-man), G. Hawkes (ironmonger), J. Hawkins (confectioner), A. G. Bartholomew (house furnisher), and S. Clifford (bootmaker).

51. 'A Kiss at the Door', Hocktide 1911. It is no longer the duty of the Tutti-men to collect rents and tithes, but other traditions have taken their place, and it is usual to demand a kiss of the lady of the house. The Tutti-men are visiting 15 High Street, and part of the shop-front of a men's outfitters can be seen on the right of the photograph (now Co-Op supermarket).

52. 'A Kiss at the Window', Hocktide *c.*1930. Sometimes extreme measures have to be taken by the Tutti-men to succeed in their aim of obtaining a kiss. Here a ladder is required to gain access to the first floor of the *Three Swans Hotel.* Co-operation and team-effort appear to have won the day!

53. *(above)* At the Workhouse, Hocktide 1913. Although it was not a property attracting Common Rights, it was usual for the Tutti-men to visit the Hungerford and Ramsbury Union Workhouse in Park Street during their journey around the town. The photograph shows some of the staff and residents greeting the Tutti-men.

54. *(above right)* At the Laundry, 1912. Another establishment frequently photographed on Tutti-day was the Hungerford Laundry in Everlands Road (see also plates 152 and 153). Not surprisingly, the standard of dress here was very high, with all the ladies wearing flowers in their hair.

55. *(right)* Shoeing the Colt, Hocktide 1913. When the business of the Hocktide Court is complete, the Commoners and their invited guests celebrate Tutti-Day with the Hocktide Lunch, previously held in the *Three Swans Hotel*, but more recently in the Corn Exchange. After lunch has been enjoyed to its full, it is traditional for all newcomers who are attending the lunch for the first time to be required to endure an initiation ceremony! Each newcomer, known as a 'colt', is shod by the local blacksmith, who hammers a horseshoe nail into his foot. The colt is only released when he shouts the 'magic' word of 'punch', and pays a contribution to his meal. The blacksmith is seen here hard at work, whilst other Commoners look on and puff at their clay pipes. The seated gentleman is holding a bowl containing the 'Plantagenet Punch', still made to a traditional recipe. It is to be hoped that the man in the foreground on the left is not the local dentist!

LAUNDRY ENTRANCE

D, HOCKTIDE

Lower High Street

56. *Three Swans Hotel* courtyard, *c.*1905. The *Three Swans Hotel* stands in the very heart of the town, and this photograph of the courtyard shows the clock-tower of the Corn Exchange above the roof line of its High Street frontage. The market-place was an ideal position for a coaching inn. Note the hand cart on the right of the yard. The *Three Swans* was one of several places where flys could be hired for travelling to neighbouring villages. The driver of the *Three Swans'* fly was Mr. Fishlock.

57. *Three Swans Hotel*, *c.*1876. This photograph is one of a series of eight splendid Cartes de Visite *c.*1875 by William Softley Parry, who was a toy dealer and photographer in Bridge Street. John Clarke Free had been innkeeper of the *Three Swans* since *c.*1850 – maybe he is one of those standing in the courtyard archway. The next building to the left is the draper's shop of Charles Robinson, this being several years before the Capital and Counties Bank redeveloped the site in the mid-1880s (now Lloyds Bank). The adjacent building on the left had been a bank since *c.*1844, when it had opened as a branch of the Wiltshire banking firm of Tanner and Pinckney, taken over by the London and County Bank *c.*1864 (now National Westminster Bank).

58. *Three Swans Hotel, c.*1900. This lantern slide shows a lady and child in a pony and trap waiting outside the *Three Swans Hotel.* On the door-case (which is in a different position to the modern entrance) is painted Francis Waldron Church, the innkeeper from *c.*1895 until the First World War. On the wall above the entrance is the badge of the Cyclists Touring Club, founded 1878. To the left is part of the Capital and Counties Bank (now Lloyds Bank). Beyond the arch to the *Three Swans* yard is the *Bell Inn*.

59. Three grocers in the Lower High Street, *c.*1920. On the left is A. J. Killick, grocer (now August Moon Chinese Restaurant). The shop-front is virtually unchanged today. The fine Queen Anne building in the centre of the photograph has already been greatly altered to accommodate the shop-front of the Reading Co-Operative Society (now Co-Op supermarket), and further down the street is the classic International Stores frontage – making three grocers within about thirty metres!

60. The post office, 14 High Street, *c.*1898. Records of the post office in Hungerford exist from as early as 1695. The post office was in Charnham Street during the coaching days of the 18th century, later moving to the High Street. From 1857-*c.*1890 it was at 25 High Street (see plate 141), when it moved to the site shown in this photograph, 14 High Street (now part of Co-Op supermarket). When telephones were first installed in Hungerford in 1907, this was the site of the first exchange. In 1914 the post office moved to newly-built premises on the opposite side of the High Street.

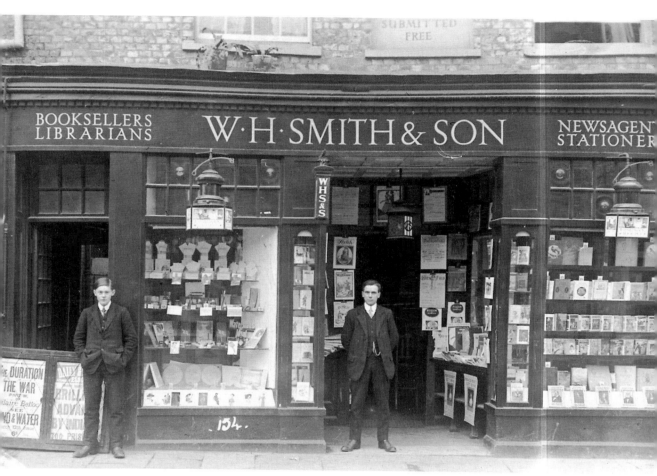

61. W. H. Smith, 6 High Street, *c.*1918. The well-known firm of W. H. Smith & Son had a shop in the High Street (now part of Martin, the newsagent) from *c.*1905. Before this, the premises had been a draper's business since the 18th century, first in the Lye family and then the Killick family. This photograph was taken by Templeman of Stoke-on-Trent, who took many war-time photographs in Hungerford.

62. Higgs, 5 High Street, and Hawkes, 3 High Street, c.1895. In the centre of the photograph is the premises of Joseph Stuart Higgs, draper here from c.1880 (now Althea's Outfitters). Another member of the family ran Higgs Bros., grocer's, at 122 High Street from c.1880 until c.1920. On the right is Samuel Hawkes – photographer, hairdresser and tobacconist (now the Tutti Pole Restaurant).

HIGH ST HUNGERFO

63. Lower High Street, c.1911. This charming photograph gives a general view, in which the buildings have changed little. There does seem to be an air of tranquillity, though, due mainly to the lack of motor cars! From the left edge of the photograph can be seen Mrs. Froome's Day and Boarding School at College House (now Freeman & Co., accountants); Thomas Fruen's china and glass shop (also the undertaker's and now Marquis Travel Agents); and Faringdon House, Dr. Walter Dickson's home and surgery (now Arosa Body Clinic).

64. Hutchins' butcher's shop, 13 High Street, c.1920. A fine display of meat is on show outside Hutchins the butcher's. Indeed, it is hard to see how one gained access to the shop with the lambs hanging over the doorway! Thomas Hutchins started the butcher's business here c.1844, and it was continued by his wife Sarah after his death. From 1906 the business was always referred to as 'Hutchins & Co.'. There was a slaughter-house behind the shop. The business was later bought by Mr. Edward Pratt, who traded until the 1960s. (It is now Knight, Frank & Rutley, estate agents, and John Lewis, pine furniture manufacturer.)

65. Bridge House, 20 June 1897. The house is shown specially decorated for Queen Victoria's Diamond Jubilee. There exists a matching photograph (not included) showing the other end of the house decorated with '1897'. Great festivities were arranged in the town to celebrate the Diamond Jubilee, and they were enjoyed to the full during a day of glorious 'Queen's' weather. With church bells, bands, processions, and a church service packed to overflowing, the morning was a continuous succession of festivities. In the afternoon, at three o'clock, a street party was organised in The Croft, with about a thousand adults and children sitting down at a long row of tables in the shade of The Avenue. At half past four, a series of sports on the Downs (the Common) was organised, ending with the Hungerford Grand National Steeplechase, from the Bath Road through two rivers and the canal at Denford to the winning post on the Downs. The day ended with a torchlit procession through the town and a bonfire and fireworks on the Downs.

The Canal

66. The canal, *c.*1906. The Western Canal was opened from Newbury to Hungerford in 1798 and eventually completed as the Kennet & Avon Canal in 1810. It was cut right through the centre of Hungerford, several houses being demolished to make way. Wilton Lodge, the house on the extreme left of the photograph, was built after the canal was completed, in 1826.

67. Hungerford wharf, *c.*1900. A wharf and grading station were established, and considerable trade flourished. Goods included gravel, chalk and whiting for the westerly route, and timber for the east. Grain and flour were carried equally in both directions. The Great Western Railway took over the canal in 1852, and trade declined, although at Hungerford 3,646 tons were loaded even as late as 1890. This photograph shows two men in a barge at the wharf, with timber and gravel nearby. The crane is clearly visible near the warehouse built of Bath stone.

68. The canal swing bridge, 1911. A peaceful summer scene, with two boys looking at the canal, and a horse waiting patiently by its laden cart. His master can be seen in silhouette in the shadow of the load. The swing bridge was on the lane joining the level crossing at the railway station with the path known aso 'Boarden Carriage' which leads to Bridge Street. It has now been replaced by an 'up and over' bridge. Behind the hay-cart can be seen the sewage pump-house, built in 1909.

69. Celebrations on the canal, 1910. This outing on a hot summer's day, with flags and parasols galore, was probably to celebrate the coronation of King George V. In the background can be seen some of the many buildings at Wooldridge's builder's yard. A pair of lock gates can be seen lying on the ground at the right edge of the picture.

70. The Quarter Mile Race, 2 August 1913. One of the main sporting features of the year was the annual Swimming Sports held at the canal wharf each summer. The popularity of this occasion can be judged from the enormous number of spectators. On the extreme left is Mr. Percy Jessett, and wearing the fireman's helmet is the Rev. Tom Gray. In the Quarter Mile Race, swimmers dived off the starting board, and swam to the Hungerford lock and back.

71. The Cigarette Race, 2 August 1913. The four contestants are 'lighting up' in readiness for the Cigarette Race! At the 'off' each swimmer had to swim to the lock and back whilst keeping a lighted cigarette in his mouth. It sounds an almost impossible task!

The Railway

72. G.W.R. station, *c.*1892. The railway first reached Hungerford in 1847, when a double track broad gauge line was extended from Newbury as the Berkshire and Hampshire Railway. The original terminus station was opened on 21 December 1847. The line was extended through the town to Seend near Devizes in November 1862, requiring considerable changes to the station, in addition to the three new bridges and embankment through the town. The original G.W.R. broad gauge track was changed to standard gauge in July 1874, but this photograph still shows the track laid on longitudinal sleepers, rather than the more familiar type seen today. This view looking west towards the town shows the station building (on the 'down' platform) before the footbridge was built (see plate 74).

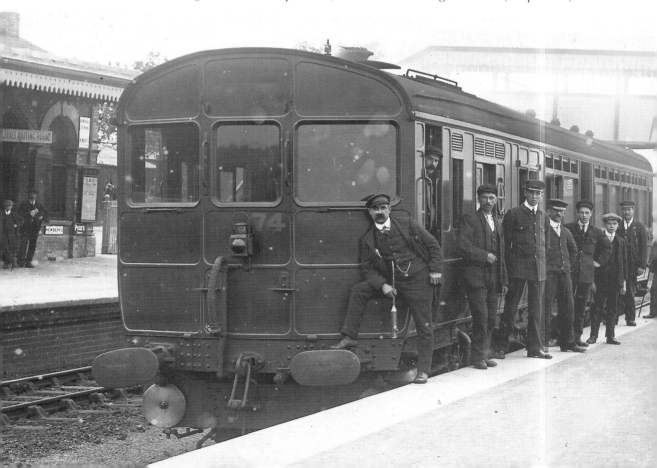

73. Hungerford Station, *c*.1916. Railway staff are standing on the 'down' platform with a pile of wicker baskets, possibly watercress crates, for which there was a very busy trade from Hungerford. Most of the station buildings were demolished in 1964, and only the footbridge remains, now without its protective canopy. The Hungerford West signal box, which can just be seen adjacent to the level crossing at the far end of the 'up' platform, was removed in 1971 after a train derailment had nearly demolished it.

74. Steam railcar at Hungerford, *c*.1912. In 1902 new station buildings were built to serve the 'up' platform, these being linked to the main station building by a footbridge. This photograph shows a steam railcar – incorporating engine and carriage in a single unit. The idea was never very successful, probably because of the limited amount of seating available. Note that the track has now been relaid on standard sleepers (see plate 72).

75. G.W.R. bus service, c.1910. To improve the service to nearby towns and villages not served by the railway, G.W.R. provided a bus connection service. Shown here is G.W.R. service no. 29, the Marlborough to Hungerford bus, which was routed via Ramsbury. The bus is a 20 h.p. Milnes Daimler, first registered in Cornwall in August 1905. The Hungerford-Marlborough service started in October 1909, and was extended to a Hungerford-Swindon service in October 1911.

76. Rossmore, Park Street, c.1920. Mr. Frank Hunt, the station-master, lived at Rossmore, the house on the junction of Station Road and Park Street, until his retirement in 1933. Mr. W. Neave Chatterton, a local dental surgeon, held a dental surgery at the house, and advertised 'Painless Extractions, Repairs at Shortest Notice, Consultations Free'. At a later date, the house was much altered, with bay windows being added at both ground – and first-floor level, and a two-floor extension to the right-hand side.

The First World War

77. Troops gather in the Market Place, *c.*1915. In January 1915, a newly-formed army unit (180 Company, Royal Army Service Corps, Mechanical Transport) arrived in Hungerford, which was to be its mobilisation station. Initially the unit was small, with one officer and 32 men, with one car, two motor-cycles and 15 lorries! The vehicles were parked in the High Street to start with, and The Croft was used as their parade ground.

78. Troops on the Common, 1915. As the size of the unit grew, the main camp was established on the Common.

79. Off to the Front, 23 July 1915. By July the unit was complete and fully prepared for battle. There were nearly 500 men and 109 vehicles. The whole company assembled in the High Street, and, watched and cheered by the whole town, they set off on their way to Avonmouth, bound for France.

80. The V.A.D. hospital, *c.*1917. During the War the old National School building (now High & Mighty, 42 High Street) was used as a convalescent hospital, for nursing wounded men who had been sent home from the Front.

81. The hospital kitchen, *c.*1917. The building was refurbished for its new use, with three small wards and a kitchen.

82. *(above)* The hospital ward, *c.*1917. There were about twenty beds, and most of the patients were Australians based at Tidworth.

83. *(top right)* Peace Celebration Dinner, Sunday 6 June 1919. The Constable, Mr. Louis Beard (of the coal yard in Bridge Street – see plate 87), arranged with the vicar, the Rev. Tom Gray, a Public Thanksgiving Service for the Return of Peace. A grand Peace Celebration Dinner was held later in the Corn Exchange.

84. *(bottom right)* The war memorial dedication service, 24 April 1921. When Hungerford selected a site for its memorial to the 76 men who died in the First World War, it chose well. The previously narrow and congested entrance to the town along Bridge Street (with the International Stores on its east side) was greatly improved by the demolition of the derelict shop and the widening of the road. The triangular strip of land between the two branches of the River Dun was landscaped, and a monument of Dolton stone, with a height of nearly seven metres, was erected. A Service of Dedication was held in April 1921, attended by a very large crowd. The High Street is seen here nearly full of people. It seems that the entire population of the town must have attended. To obtain enough height for this photograph, Albert Parsons must have stood on the bridge parapet – a pretty hazardous position with so many about!

PEACE CELEBRATION DINNER
JULY 1919

85. Getting as near as possible. Few of those attending could possibly have heard the words spoken by the Rev. Mr. Gray and the dignitaries taking the service. Many of those standing in Bridge Street, some of whom had brought their bicycles, would just have had to watch in silence. In the background is the Wesleyan chapel in Charnham Street (now Meadowview Squash Club and Chapel Court).

86. 'In humble gratitude and loving memory'. This 'bird's-eye' view of the service in progress clearly shows the island in Bridge Street on which the old Priory of St John stood in medieval times.

Bridge Street

87. Bridge Street from the canal bridge, 1910. On the extreme right is Beard's coal-merchants, started by John Beard in the 1840s (now Harlequin Antiques). The horse and cart is standing outside the barber's shop run by Mr. Francis Batt (now Hodgers of Hungerford fashions). He also ran the *Barley Mow*, an inn established *c.*1830 (now Stirland's garage). The shop on the left of Bridge Street, with a blind over the pavement, was a confectioner's run by the Phelps family. George Phelps and later his son George Thomas, affectionately known as 'Gingerbread Phelps', ran the bakery, grocery, and confectionery business until the First World War. The shop was subsequently used by Charles Batchelor as a café and confectioner's; Earle's Stores as an ironmonger's; Free's as a furniture shop; and since 1978 by Roxton Sporting Ltd. Beyond Mill Cottage (the white-fronted half-hipped building) can be seen the Town Mill (see plate 88).

88. Town Mill, *c.*1900. Opposite the *John of Gaunt Inn* was the Town Mill, once known as Queen's Mill. We know that there were two water mills in the town in 1275, and one of them was probably on this site. The miller's cottage is on the left of the picture (now Mill Cottage). In the early years of this century the miller was Robert Cole (who later moved to 104 High Street). The mill closed *c.*1914 and was demolished in 1935, when a private house (Mill Hatch) was built on the site. Beyond the mill can be seen Rumball's butcher's shop. The butcher's business was started *c.*1860 by William Cruse, and Ernest Rumball took over *c.*1896. (Now Paravicini, art dealer and antiques.)

89. Bridge Street towards Bear Corner, *c.*1907. Until *c.*1740 the main entrance to the town from the Bath Road had been through a ford in the River Dun, where the railings are on the right edge of this photograph. There were so many complaints about poor access that land was purchased from the *Bear Inn*, and a new road and two bridges were built to bring the road directly from the *Bear* across the island on which the Priory of St John had stood some centuries earlier. This is still the line of the present road, and explains why there is such a sharp corner in the middle of Bridge Street near the *John of Gaunt Inn*. On the left is Freeman Brothers' shop (tobacconists, fishing tackle and fancy goods) who published a number of the photographs used in this book; on the right is the International Stores.

90. International Stores, *c.*1912. This shop was on the east side of Bridge Street, on what is now the War Memorial Gardens. The shop clearly thrived through the early years of the century, and a series of similar formal photographs were taken over several years. After the First World War, however, the International Stores moved to the High Street, and this site was cleared for the war memorial in 1920.

91. Bridge Street and war memorial, *c.*1921. After the demolition of the International Stores and the building of the new war memorial, Bridge Street gained a quite new and spacious feel, providing a far better entrance to the town.

92. Hungerford Printing Works, 2 Bridge Street, 1912. William Franklin, printer, bookseller, auctioneer and registrar of births, marriages and deaths, ran his business from this shop from *c.*1841 until his death *c.*1865. His widow, Mary, then continued until it was bought by Alfred New *c.*1881. Mr. E. W. Munford came from Huntingdonshire, and was apprenticed in London before coming to Hungerford in 1912. He continued the printing business here until *c.*1919, when he moved to 129 High Street. It is interesting that he appears to have swapped premises at this time with Tom Fruen, the china and glass dealer (also an undertaker), who moved from 129 High Street down to 2 Bridge Street, where he stayed until 1933. (This is now Michael Macklin, framemakers.)

93. Tanyard Lawn, *c*.1912. This photograph was taken from an upstairs room of Albert Parsons' Bridge Street studio (see plate 125). The view shows the *Bear Hotel* on the left, the Wesleyan chapel in the middle, and on the extreme right is the splendid Georgian house called Riverside, built *c*.1810 (now Riverside Antiques). This had been the site of Hungerford's tannery since at least 1640, and it continued as such until 1886.

The lawn shown on this picture was known as Tanyard Lawn, although it had originally belonged to the *Bear*. Before 1740 the old road into the town passed immediately in front of the tannery building and linked with Bridge Street through a ford of the River Dun. The right of way along the old road was not closed until 1912. The Tanyard chimney was demolished *c*.1908.

Charnham Street

94. Bear Corner and Charnham Street, 1903. This view looks west from the Bear Corner: Over the front entrance of the *Bear* can be seen the name of Edith Osmond, who ran the inn for only a few years around the turn of the century. The Triumph cycle advert on the right is on the wall of Stradling's cycle shop (see plate 97).

95. Charnham Street, *c*.1906. A fine summer day has brought many people out in their 'Sunday best'. Perched somewhat precariously on the bicycle is a young child. The text of the postcard includes the comment: 'What do you think of your little Tommy here?!' The *Sun Inn* was run at this time by Mr. Francis Jessett, member of a large Hungerford family.

96. Charnham Street, *c*.1919. On the extreme left is The Hungerford Gas Company showroom (now Below Stairs showroom). Beyond it are the premises of John Waller Horne (now Unwin & Davis, newsagent), described in *Kelly's* directories of 1903 and 1911 as 'carman and jobmaster', with horses and traps to let or hire. In 1895, he was at the *Plough Inn* in the High Street (see plate 127), where he hired 'waggonettes and traps'.

97. W. H. Giles, Hungerford carrier, *c.*1918. The dozen or so local carriers fulfilled a vital role in the community, providing a link with adjacent towns and villages in the days before any 'public' transport. One Hungerford carrier was William Harry Giles, who provided carriage to Newbury three days a week from 1903. He is photographed here with his sons Harry (standing) and Percy (in the driving seat), and their Daimler coach. The photograph is taken outside the premises of Stradling & Plenty (now Roberta hair salon) next to the Wesleyan chapel in Charnham Street.

98. Wesleyan chapel, Charnham Street, *c*.1910. The Wesleyan chapel was built in 1869 at a cost of about £3,000. It stood on the site of the *White Hart Inn* (which traded from 1686 until 1864), opposite the *Bear*, and therefore occupied a prominent position in the town until it was demolished in 1971. The site has now been redeveloped for Chapel Court and the Meadowview Squash Club.

99. Charnham Street, 1906. Beyond the cottages on the left (long since demolished) can be seen the *Red Lion* (now Toad and Trout Bistro), advertising Finn's Genuine Ales and Stout. In the foreground on the right is one of the crooked-shape water pipes, used to supply water-carts which damped down the dusty roads in dry weather. There were several other water pipes around the town, some of which can be seen in this book; they were installed *c*.1904 and were used until the main roads in the town were macadamised. One resident recalls that 'the sound of the watering-cart going up and down the street heralded to us children the start of summer'.

100. Faulknor Square, *c.*1912. This lovely square is seen in this photograph as a splendid private grassed area, screened from Bath Road by a tall well-trimmed hedge. Both the south and west terraces seen here were built *c.*1740, although they have interesting differences in detail.

The Fire Brigade

101. The first steam fire engine, *c.*1908. The original hand-operated fire pump had been kept in the Town Hall during the 19th century, but in 1891 the town acquired its first steam fire pump, a 'Greenwich', made by the firm of Merryweather. The pump was horse-drawn and suffered from a number of idiosyncrasies, so it required special skills to operate the engine successfully! These were well mastered by the newly-formed Volunteer Fire Brigade, and on 18 November 1891 a public demonstration of the new Greenwich machine was staged at the Town Hall. Four fine horses hauled the engine at a gallop along the street from the fire station in Charnham Street to the canal wharf. One thousand feet of hose was extended up the street, and within seven and a half minutes, the pump was at full pressure, and able to throw a jet of water 30 or 40 ft. over the Town Hall. When tested back at the wharf, it achieved a jet of about 150 ft., and the admiring crowds cheered enthusiastically. To celebrate the event a dinner was held in the Corn Exchange, about a hundred gentlemen being present. This photograph (probably at Denford Mill) shows the Greenwich engine being tested by Mr. Alfred Macklin (left) and Mr. Harry Champ.

102. The H.V.F.B. at the fire station, c.1891. To accommodate the new Greenwich fire engine, the town's first fire station was built in Charnham Street, adjacent to Faulknor Square. On the left is Mr. George Platt (of the town brewery, who gave the premises adjacent to the tannery for use as the fire station); George Cottrell (the Captain of the Brigade, and owner of Cottrell's Iron Works in Eddington); the branchmen were Messrs. Beard, Hoskings, Alexander and Jessett; the firemen were Messrs. Astley, Cundell, Adnams and Killick; chief engineer was Mr. W. Sperring, and his assistant was Mr. Dear.

103. The Dreadnought fire engine, 1910. Good though the Greenwich fire engine had been, technology was rapidly advancing, and the need for a self-propelled machine was evident. In 1910 the town took possession of a new and more powerful Merryweather steam fire engine, named 'The Dreadnought'. This photograph shows the scene at the fire station on the hand-over day. The driver is one of Merryweather's own staff, but the entire brigade has managed to climb aboard. Mr. George Cottrell (the Captain of the Brigade) is sitting on the driver's left, and the Rev. Tom Gray is on his right. Note the lights, the fire-bell and the solid tyres.

104. Preparing for the Grand Demonstration, 1910. Remembering the fine demonstration put on in 1891 when the previous engine had been delivered, the fire brigade arranged a similar demonstration at the wharf, attended by a large crowd of town officials and the general public. Final preparations are well in hand; the inlet hose is already in the canal.

105. Demonstrating The Dreadnought, 1910. 'The Power of the Pump was Marvellous to Behold!' The town was justifiably proud of its new acquisition, and the wharf, with a ready supply of water, proved to be a perfect arena for the very large crowd who gathered. The engine could travel at speeds up to 30 m.p.h., deliver 300 gallons of water per minute, and send a jet of water 150 ft. into the air. Several of the wharf buildings can be seen in the background.

106. Funeral of Mr. F. R. Pratt, 9 June 1910. In the same year that the new fire engine came to Hungerford, one of the brigade members, Mr. F. R. Pratt, landlord of the *Bear Hotel*, was killed in a road traffic accident. A grand funeral was arranged, with his colleagues in the fire brigade pulling the funeral carriage from the *Bear* along Charnham Street to St Saviour's church in Eddington. This photograph shows the funeral procession passing Faulknor Square. On the left is Alec Townsin's Refreshment Rooms (now Bow House Antiques) in Faulknor Square, then the fire station (now the Fire Place), with the *Bear Hotel* in the distance. On the right is James Stradling's cycle shop, a business founded in Newbury in 1877 (now Fires and Grates), and the *Red Lion Inn*.

Eddington

107. Eddington from Eddington Bridge, 1915. A bridge over the Kennet at Hungerford was mentioned as long ago as 1275. Lying on the northern bank of the River Kennet, Eddington was a self-contained village, with its own post office, shops, church, garage, inn, infant school and iron-works providing plenty of local employment.

108. Oxford Street, Eddington, c.1911. Taken from the main road looking north towards Linden Cottage, this photograph shows the Eddington post office on the right (now a private house), opposite which is a terrace of cottages with interesting decorative brickwork (demolished 1966 before the building of Kennet Court). Beyond the post office is one of Hungerford's very early garages, with the name Hillsdon & Co., Eddington Motor Works, previously the Infant National School from 1869 (6 Oxford Street, now a private house). Mr. C. O. Hillsdon lived next door at Buckland House.

109. *(above)* Eddington post office, *c*.1907. Trade directories as far back as 1844 mention the Jessett family grocery shop in Eddington. The business passed from Francis to George to Mrs. Jane Jessett and, *c*.1891 to Mr. Frederick Jessett, whose shop it was at the time of this photograph. The family lived in the house, behind which was the large bakery. Other members of this large family-owned shops in other parts of Hungerford, for example, in *Kelly's* of 1920 we find Francis Jessett, the *Sun* public house, Charnham Street; Frederick Jessett, baker, Charnham Street; and Thomas Jessett, beer retailer, Park Street. The Victorian post-box in the wall of the building is still in use today. On the left can be seen Mr. Lewington's coal cart on its rounds.

110. *(above right)* Jessett's bakery, 1915. During the First World War, Frederick Jessett supplied bread to the troops stationed at Hungerford (see plates 77-79). The photograph shows many dozen loaves of various shapes and sizes, ready to be delivered to the army.

111. *(right)* Supplying bread to the troops, 1915. It seems that the regular deliveries of bread to the army on the Common were made by commissioning a furniture wagon. An officer can be seen checking the delivery against his order form.

F. JESSETT
BAKERS
ARMY CONTRACTOR
EDDINGTON.
HUNGERFORD

112. Oxford Street, *c.*1912. The grocery shop on the right was run by two Misses Winkworth, and although now a private house, the 'shop' window and doorway are unchanged today. On the left is a group of workers at the wheelwright and blacksmith, including Norman Higgins (blacksmith), Jim Middleton (carpenter) and Bill Wiggins (blacksmith). At the far end of this part of Oxford Street is Linden Cottage, where the road turns left towards Eddington Bridge.

113. Folly Hill, *c.*1908. The buildings are little different today, with Hansel's Cottage on the left and St Saviour's church partly hidden by The Hermitage on the right. The road was widened at this point during the 1970s to accommodate the heavy use made of this trunk road.

114. St Saviour's church, Eddington, *c.*1920. This church was built 'for the convenience of the northern part of the parish' and opened in 1868. The land was given by William Honywood of Chilton Lodge, and the church was built by the local firm of Thomas Wooldridge at a cost of £2,000. It is in the Early English style and was designed by Sir Arthur Blomfield. Standing on high ground overlooking the Kennet valley and the town of Hungerford, the churchyard to the north of the church is still used as the parish burial ground.

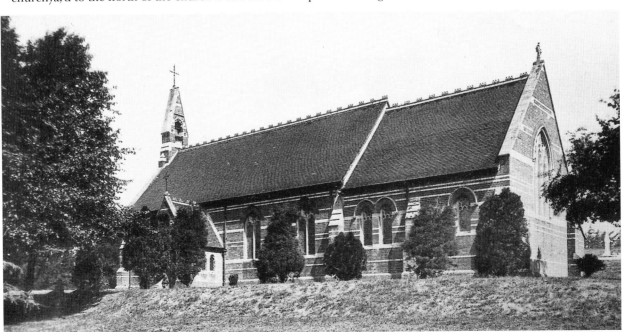

115. St Saviour's church, c.1920. The church seated 250 people, and was in regular use for over 100 years until it closed c.1970. It was converted into a private house (Church House) in 1977.

116. Eddington turnpike gate c.1850. The Eddington turnpike is thought to have been on Folly Hill, the road north from Eddington towards Shefford and Wantage, and the gate is possibly at the junction with the Upper Eddington Road, opposite the gate to St Saviour's church. If the gatekeeper lived in the tiny cottage with his family, then it must indeed have been crowded, as there are at least nine people in the photograph!

117. Cottrell, Rose & Co. Ltd., 1903. There were two large iron founders in Hungerford at the turn of the century. One of these was George Cottrell's Iron Works in Eddington, established c.1869. Their entry in *Kelly's Directory* describes them as 'iron founders, millwrights, agricultural implement and boiler makers; patentees of the "Climax" (gold medal) folding elevator and prize medal engines and water carts'. The firm closed c.1911 and few of the original buildings remain now.

118. Cottrell, Rose & Co., catalogue, 1897. The goods on offer seem to be remarkable value for money, with the Improved One Horse Cart selling for £15 0s. 0d. and the award winning 'Climax' Elevator just £42 0s. 0d.

COTTRELL, ROSE & Co., Ltd., Eddington Iron Works, HUNGERFORD, Berks.

IMPROVED FARM CART.

This Cart is well adapted for all farm and general purposes, the body being roomy and strongly framed together of well-seasoned English timber, and fitted with improved tipping arrangement.

PRICES.

	£	s.	d.
Strong One Horse Cart, with 3in. wheels	15	0	0
Head and Tail Ladders, extra	1	10	0

LONDON PATTERN HAY CART

A useful and roomy Cart, with oak frame, plank sides, fitted with tipping apparatus, wheels 5ft. high, with hay ladder over horse, and projecting ladder at back.

Price £19 0 0

Designs upon Application.

Illustrated General Catalogues sent free on application to

COTTRELL, ROSE & Co., Ltd.,

EDDINGTON IRON AND WAGON WORKS,

HUNGERFORD,

BERKS., ENGLAND.

"CLIMAX"

FOLDING ELEVATOR.

New Arrangement for Lifting Troughs when Topping-up Hay Ricks, &c.

These Engravings represent our New Patent "Climax" Elevator, with gearing and attachments for raising troughs bodily over the rick when topping-up, thus dispensing with the usual pitch-hole, and pronounced by Agriculturists to be a great improvement. The hopper is hung on pivots, and is adjustable to the position of troughs.

FIRST PRIZE,
GOLD MEDAL,
AMSTERDAM, 1884.

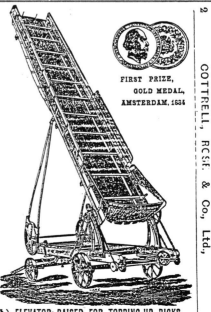

COTTRELL, ROSE & Co., Ltd.,

PRICES.

	£	s.	d.
Round Hopper Elevator, with lifting arrangement (30ft. high)	49	10	0
Angular Gear, as above	2	10	0
Horse Gear	7	0	0

(30ft.) ELEVATOR RAISED FOR RICK BUILDING.

(30ft.) ELEVATOR RAISED FOR TOPPING-UP RICKS.

119. Eddington Garage, c.1922. After Cottrell's Iron Works closed, the site was used as a motor business, initially called Eddington Garage. In 1922 it was bought by Bill Norman, and the business ran under the name of Norman's Garage until 1970. This photograph is taken looking north across the forecourt. (It is now Petropolis petrol station.)

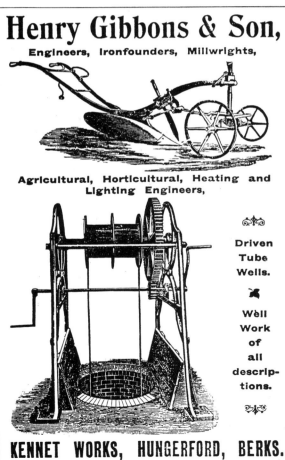

Henry Gibbons & Son,

Engineers, Ironfounders, Millwrights,

Agricultural, Horticultural, Heating and Lighting Engineers,

Driven Tube Wells.

Well Work of all descriptions.

KENNET WORKS, HUNGERFORD, BERKS.

120. Henry Gibbons & Son, catalogue, c.1895. Not to be outdone by their competitors, the other local engineering firm of Henry Gibbons & Son, of the Kennet Works in Charnham Street (now Riverside petrol station) advertised themselves as 'manufacturer of Gibbons' patent moulding machines, lawn mower sharpeners, patent safety flush bolts and manufacturers of steam and hot water fittings and all kinds of agricultural implements (medals awarded)'. This firm had been established by Richard Gibbons at Ramsbury in 1814. He moved to 16 Bridge Street, Hungerford, in 1824 before building a new foundry in Charnham Street in 1839.

121. Kennet Motor Works, *c*.1939. Henry Gibbons Engineering Works closed in 1931, the site being taken over as the Kennet Motor Works in 1936 by Mr. Ludford. The business was quite a large one for the period, with five petrol pumps on the forecourt. In the photograph are the Maxwell breakdown truck, an Austin Seven and an Austin Ten. The pump price of Cleveland petrol was 1s. 7d. per gallon.

Portraits

122. Edward Bushnell, Bellman, c.1920. Mr. Edward Bushnell was Town Crier from 1880 until 1923. He ran a coffee tavern at 3 High Street (now the Tutti Pole Restaurant), and was responsible for the running of the Town Hall and Corn Exchange. Amongst many other duties, he was responsible for ringing the fire bell on the roof of the Town Hall in the event of a fire, for which he was paid 5s. 0d. – a considerable sum at the time. He was succeeded in his role of Bellman and Town Crier by his son Sydney Bushnell, and later by the present bellman, Robin Tubb, who is Edward Bushnell's great-grandson. The office of Bellman has therefore been held by the same family in Hungerford for well over a century.

123. Tom Gray, c.1920. The Reverend William Edward Thomas Seccombe Gray was always known as Tom. He was vicar of Hungerford from 1909 until 1924, and was much involved in the community life of the town during the years covered by many of the photographs in this book. He was a very popular man and a keen sportsman, fishing and shooting being his special interests. Indeed, he wrote a book on fishing under the pen-name 'Silver Devon' entitled *Leaves from an Anglers Notebook*. He was an active member of the Hungerford Volunteer Fire Brigade, rising to the most senior rank of Captain, and skilfully managed to combine a 'dog-collar' with his fireman's uniform!

Albert Parsons

124. Albert Parsons, *c*.1914. A large number of the photographs in this book were taken by one photographer, Albert Parsons, who came to Hungerford in *c*.1902. The quality of his work is second to none, and his output was prolific. He is shown here as proud owner of his 1908 Rover 6 h.p. car, which was produced in dark green paintwork, with dark red upholstery, and capable of speeds of up to 50 m.p.h.! The vehicle was fitted with *two* brake pedals, whilst speed was controlled by hand rather than by a foot pedal.

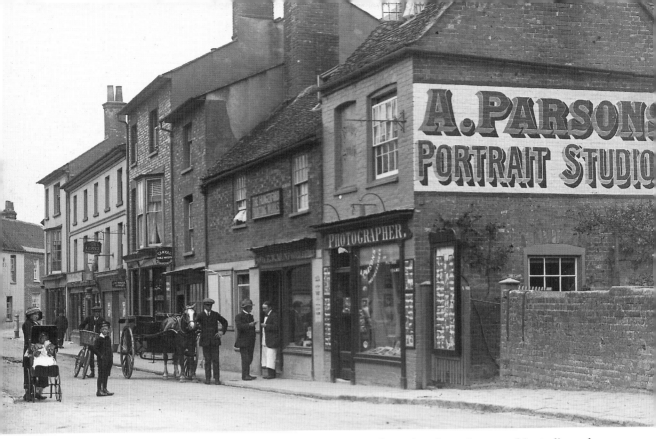

125. Bridge Street, *c.*1914. Initially Mr. Parsons was unable to find ideal premises for a photographic studio, so he and his wife made their first home in Church Street, and built a studio in the garden. Within a few years, however, he was able to move to a prime site at 1 Bridge Street, next to the Hungerford Printing Works.

126. Upper High Street, *c.*1918. Albert Parsons joined the Royal Flying Corps during the war, and soon after his return home the family moved to 30 High Street (Barclays Bank), premises previously owned by William Mapson, a watch-maker and photographer who had worked there since 1891. He later expanded his business to include car hire. The photograph shows the studio on the extreme right, with his car standing outside. When Albert Parsons died in 1950, the business closed, and the property was used as the Gateway Café (run by Miss Catherine Rose) until being redeveloped by Barclays Bank, which opened in 1967.

Upper High Street

127. The *Plough Inn*, 49 High Street, *c.*1910. There were three inns near the top of the High Street: the *Salisbury Arms*, the *Borough Arms* (now the *Tuttiman*), and the *Plough*. The *Plough* dated from *c.*1854, and closed around the First World War (now residential).

128. Upper High Street, 1915. The horse and cart in the distance are collecting water from the pump at Atherton field, later Atherton Crescent. On the left are the cottages which were later demolished to make way for the High Street flats called Fairfields.

129. Salisbury Road, *c.*1910. Moving now to the southern limits of the town, this photograph shows the view looking back towards the town. On the left is Church Way, and with very few buildings to block the view, the new Council School (built 1910) is clearly visible on the high ground of Fairview Road. Just visible down the hill is the St John's Mission Hall (see plate 130).

130. Interior of St John's Mission Hall, *c.*1910. The Mission Hall was built in 1899, funded by Lady Pearce (of Chilton Lodge). It was run by the Church Army, and was under the care of Captain Birt (and from 1920 by Captain Robert Manfield and his sister). In addition to the regular services, regular 'Band of Cheer' sessions were held every Wednesday afternoon, when a bun and cup of tea would cost 1d. The hall was also used on numerous occasions for whist drives, concerts, and other activities. This photograph was clearly taken at Harvest Thanksgiving, and the man on the right of the photograph is thought to be Captain Birt, shown with his family.

131. Gathering barley in Atherton field, 1909. This splendid photograph shows the Macklin family and helpers. The field had earlier belonged to Lady Atherton, who is said to have offered the field to the town as a cemetery. This plan was not followed through, however, and Atherton Crescent, a fine curved line of houses set well back from the main road, was built in 1921.

132. Upper High Street, *c.*1905. The steam traction engine stands outside the *Salisbury Arms* which traded from *c.*1850 until after the Second World War. The High Street narrows at this point, which represents the southern limit of the town before the 19th century. There was a boundary gate across the road here until the early 19th century.

133. Upper High Street, 1910. The lady on the left is standing in the doorway of Alfred Mills, butcher's. The next shop was Ernest W. Batt, bakery and cake shop.

134. W. H. Giles, 43 High Street, c.1908. William Harry Giles, the Hungerford carrier, lived and worked from 43 High Street, adjacent to the National School. His younger son Percy is shown here holding the horse, and sitting on the cart are his elder son Harry (holding the whip) and Bob Newhook.

135. Macklin's Dairy, 89 High Street, *c.*1905. Mr. Frederick Macklin is seen here sitting in his wagonette outside his dairy in the High Street (now T. Jefferies & Son, Devonia Bakery). The driver is his son Alfred Macklin. On the driver's seat support is the Hungerford crest and the name 'Eclipse'. Mr. Macklin used to lead the cows from the Common down Cow Lane (Park Street) and up the High Street to the dairy for milking.

136. Upper High Street, 1911. The bicycle on the left is leaning against William Harris' baker's and grocer's shop. The business had started *c*.1865, and closed in 1956. Behind the brick wall to the right of the bakery was a blacksmith's yard (now the Launderama).

137. Clifford's, 110 High Street, *c*.1928. The shop sign says that Clifford's boot and shoe business was established in 1700. Records show that in 1869 Stephen Clifford ran a boot and shoemaking business in Charnham Street, and that it moved to 110 High Street (now Hants and Berks Property, estate agents), *c*.1896. The shopkeeper in this photograph is Stephen's son, William Martin Clifford, who ran the business from *c*.1920 until it closed in 1966. Advertisements in the window include Wren's polish, Blanco, Brook's Dye Works in Bristol, K Shoes and Boots, and Comac Shoes.

138. Adnams' Corn Merchants, 28 High Street, 1912. John Corderoy Adnams ran a seed and corn merchant business from this property from the 1870s. He lived in the main part of the house, with the shop on the right-hand side. The building is shown decorated for the King's visit of 1912 (see plates 156-170). In 1960 the local solicitors' firm of Charles Lucas and Marshall moved here from Bridge Villa (see plate 65), and the shop front was removed. Adnams' mill was set back behind this building, and part of it is now converted to flats known as The Granary.

139. Market Place, c.1876. This photograph is one of a series of eight Cartes de Visite of Hungerford by W. S. Parry of Bridge Street (see also plate 57), and shows an important group of buildings in the Market Place. From left to right can be seen Thomas Alexander's grocer's shop (and his house), the post office, Henry Wren's ironmonger's and saddler's, Keen's brewery and the Town Hall.

140. Alexander's Stores, 27 High Street, *c.*1912. This timber-framed building is one of the oldest in Hungerford. Thomas Alexander took over the family business in *c.*1865, and his son, Thomas Walter Alexander, followed him in *c.*1895, and traded until 1946. It has been Hungerford Antiques Arcade since 1972.

141. London & Provincial Stores, 25 High Street, *c.*1900. Alexander's heavy coal waggon, with Bill Lewington holding the reins, is standing outside the London & Provincial Stores (until recently Spackman's grocer's). The building has a long and interesting history, having been owned by (amongst others) a doctor and a bishop before becoming a draper's shop. In *c.*1857 it was Hungerford's post office, when Charles Osmond was postmaster. At the end of the century it began a long period as a food shop, first as the London & Provincial Stores (shown here), then *c.*1911 as Edward Gingell's Family Grocers, before being bought by Philip Spackman in 1949.

142. Wren's, ironmonger and saddler, 24 High Street, *c*.1891. This timber-framed building overlooking the Market Place was the *Greyhound Inn* in the 18th century. William Alexander opened a saddler's business in part of the building in 1813, and in 1865 Henry Wren and John Matthews expanded it to include ironmongery. Henry Wren died in 1890, and his brother George Wren inherited the property. This photograph was probably taken soon after the change of ownership. On the left are (from left to right) Frederick Rosier (saddler) and George Wren (owner); in the middle are the tinsmith, Mr. Tidbury (an apprentice saddler), and, in the apron, Mr. Gregory (a saddler). On the right are two (unknown) saddlers. The window displays illustrate the extensive range of hardware goods for sale, and on the pavement are garden tools and a variety of harness, saddles, and leather bags. There is a lady standing at the right-hand first-floor window. Perhaps she is George Wren's wife. (This is now Supernews newsagents, Hungerford Wine Company, and The Courtyard.)

143. The Market Place, *c*.1895. This early view of the Market Place shows (from left to right): George Wren's ironmonger's and saddler's, Elisha Love's Crown Brewery, the Town Hall and Corn Exchange, Frederick Barnard's fishmongers, and Ernest Barnard's furniture shop. Note the old front on the Crown Brewery, and the two small shop fronts on Barnard's premises.

144. The Market Place, 1902. There are interesting changes from the previous photograph: by 1902 the Crown Brewery had been re-roofed and re-fronted in mock-Tudor style, and the shops to the right of the Corn Exchange had been refitted with a new three-bay shop front.

145. Barnard's Stationers, 21 High Street, *c.*1925. Some years later again, the middle and right of the three shops had been swapped, and it was the middle of the three which was now Ernest Barnard's newsagent, stationery, fancy goods and tobacconist shop. Note the fine pair of gas lamps hanging outside. Adverts include Slazenger rackets and balls, Maharaja cigars, and the *Newbury Weekly News* which was reporting Town Council elections. (It is now Unwin's wine merchant.)

Schools

THE NEW SCHOOLS
HUNGERFORD, 1910

146. Council School, 1910. In September 1910 a fine new all-age school was built in Fairview Road, replacing the National School (in the High Street) and the Wesleyan School (in Church Street). This photograph was taken from Atherton Hill, looking over the roof tops of Salisbury Row. The main building was for children aged six to fourteen years, and the smaller building on the left was for the infants, aged three to five years. The design incorporated the most modern features of its time, including central heating, running water and flush toilets, facilities which were not yet available in many private houses in the town.

147. Nature pond, *c.*1920. The children were encouraged to study nature, and they built a small pond in the school grounds so that they could keep some of the plants and animals gathered from the countryside. Some buildings in Fairview Road can be seen in the background. The teacher in this photograph is Miss Waddington.

148. Boys' gardening class, c.1925. In a thoroughly practical way, the curriculum included gardening classes for boys. Note the town crest proudly displayed on the roof of the shed.

149. Mr. Camburn's retirement, 1921. The first headmaster of the new Council School was Mr. Caleb Camburn. He had previously been headmaster of the Wesleyan School in Church Street from 1886. Under his portrait can be seen the school initials (H.C.S. – Hungerford Council School), the Hungerford town crest (star and crescent), the school motto (devised by Mr. Camburn) 'No Quest, No Conquest', and the old county badge of Royal Berkshire depicting a stag under a tree. Behind the group of children can be seen the newly-built houses in Atherton Crescent, and a pair of cottages in Church Way.

The Police

150. The police station, *c*.1910. The police station in Park Street was built in 1864, and is still used today. Although the interior has been much altered, the appearance of the building is virtually unchanged.

151. The police reserve, 1919. There are no fewer than 33 men in this photograph, nearly all of them with a moustache, and one of them, the Rev. Mr. Denning, with a 'dog-collar'. The formal group photograph is taken at the entrance to the police station. Note the roses and ivy on the walls, and the geraniums and clipped box hedges in the gardens.

The Laundry

152. Hungerford Laundry, *c.*1910. The Hungerford Sanitary Laundry Co. Ltd. was established *c.*1908, and took over the large brewery building in Everland Road. The latest equipment was installed, and the firm enjoyed a reputation for the high quality of its work. A report on a visit to the laundry states: 'After inspecting this establishment, I can honestly certify that from the receiving room to the despatch room every detail has been carefully studied, and no expense has been spared to make it a thoroughly up-to-date sanitary laundry, and the motto of the company has been carried out to the letter, viz.: Cleanliness, Efficiency, and Sanitation'. The price list includes ladies bodice (3d.); silk stockings (3d.); d'oyley (1¼ d.); ladies' knickers (3½ d. to 6d.); whilst maids' knickers were only 2½ d! This photograph shows the ironing room of the laundry and gives some idea of the large scale of the operation.

153. Hungerford Laundry delivery team, c.1910. A large team of men and horses was required to collect and deliver laundry around the area. Some of them are pictured here in the stable yard. The laundry closed in December 1966 after several changes of ownership, having been renamed The Rose of Hungerford Laundry in the 1950s. (It is now Loheat Ltd.)

Church Street

154. Church Street, 1915. This scene at the corner of Croft Road has changed little, apart from the absence nowadays of the iron railings.

155. James' Great Western Mill, *c.*1930. The family milling business of James & Co. was a large employer in the town. Having started at the water mill in Chilton Foliat, they moved in 1926 to part of the old brewery in Everlands Road, whilst building a new mill in Church Street. This Great Western Mill opened in 1930. In June 1960, however, the mill caught fire, and overnight the building was totally destroyed. A new James' Mill was built at Smitham Bridge (demolished in 1986 for housing development) and the Church Street site was made available for the present library (1967), fire station (1968), and car-park.

King's Visit—21-26 October 1912

156. The King's visit, 21-26 October 1912. In October 1912 King George V visited Sir John Ward at Chilton Lodge. The proposed visit captured the enthusiasm of the whole town, which set about the task of preparing and decorating the town with enormous energy. Albert Parsons took the opportunity to photograph every part of the town, and as a result we now have a very full record of a day in the life of Hungerford. This photograph shows Mr. Frank Hunt, the station-master of the G.W.R. station, with his staff (no fewer than 26 men at the time).

157. The Constable and Feoffees. The town officials were all on parade to welcome His Majesty, and are photographed here at the railway station awaiting his arrival. They include (from left to right) Messrs. E. Bushnell (Town Crier), F. W. Church (landlord of *Three Swans Hotel*), Freeman (tobacconist), G. Platt (brewer), T. Alexander, H. d'O. W. Astley, J. Adnams (Constable), G. Wren, A. Allright, T. W. Alexander, L. Beard (in Burberry coat), W. Mapson, and (on the extreme right) Mr. F. Hunt (station-master).

158. The King on the way to the station. The day of the King's departure from Hungerford was spoiled by heavy rain. Despite this, the band (on the left) played on, and a large crowd came to cheer. Sadly the profusion of umbrellas must have reduced the view considerably. The King's journey to Hungerford had been non-stop from Paddington, and took an hour and ten minutes, arriving at 7.15 p.m. He left at 10.40 a.m. on Saturday 26 October.

159. The Market Place. Bunting and flags were everywhere, with every shop festooned. Note the very tall telegraph poles, carrying the wires high above the railway bridge.

160. The Lower High Street. From left to right can be seen Allright's Universal Stores, the post office and Hutchin & Co., butchers.

161. Manor House and the Lower High Street. On the right of this photograph is the Manor House, where Dr. Blake James lived and held his surgery. This was to be the doctors' surgery until 1959, when a new surgery was built in The Croft. Manor House was demolished in 1965 to make way for a petrol filling station (now Gateway supermarket). To the left of Manor House can be seen Arthur Higgs' grocer's shop (now Rayner's optician's and Inklings gift shop); John Tyler's draper's and milliner's shop (now Barnaby's bread and confectionery); Arthur Bingham's chemist shop (now Packwood's pharmacy); and Earle's Ironmonger's Store (now the post office building).

162. The triumphal arch and canal bridge. The sign to the left of the bridge, near the two children, advertises 'Umbrellas Made, Recovered and Repaired'.

163. The canal bridge. Note the gas lamps on the bridge, and the patriotic welcome 'God Bless You and Yours'.

164. The triumphal arch and Lower High Street. Preparations are still in hand, with ladders in place against the triumphal arch.

VISIT OF THE KING TO HUNGERFORD. 21.10.12

165. *(left)* Bridge Street. On the left is the entrance to the canal wharf. The wharf had been run by Mr. Thomas Wooldridge, and later by his son John Holmes Wooldridge. In addition to the trade on the canal, they also ran a builder's business here, and were widely acclaimed especially for their work in church restoration. The family lived at 13 Bridge Street (now Blakeway Books) and the builder's business continued to operate until 1967. The redevelopment of the wharf and Canal Walk took place in 1973.

166. *(below left)* Bridge Street and International Stores. On the right is the International Stores. Note how it narrowed the road at this point.

167. *(below)* Bridge Street from Bear Corner. The River Dun in Bridge Street marked the county boundary between Wiltshire and Berkshire until boundary changes of 1894. The banner reminds us of this with the message 'Welcome to the Royal County'.

168. Agricultural arch by the *Sun Inn*. Perhaps the finest decoration of all was the magnificent agricultural arch, built adjacent to the *Sun Inn* in Charnham Street. H. Gibbons and Son now describe themselves on the advertising board as 'General Engineers', but their agricultural origins are evident from the arch. It contains examples of their craft, including scythes, ploughs, and harrows, all artistically combined on two of their famous grain elevators.

169. Agricultural arch with staff of Gibbons Ironworks. It was a splendid exhibition, and the staff of Gibbons were understandably proud of their achievement, happily posing for a formal photograph under their arch.

170. The Bear Corner. The final photograph of the book brings us full circle, showing the scene at the Bear Corner. Note the A.A. man standing near the signpost. The *Bear* now advertises itself as a 'family hotel' with 'spacious garage'. The age of the car had begun in Hungerford!

Thank you Tony & Stella for being such
good neighbours over the years.
Love & all good wishes Beth & Richard.

All the very best in your new life - Mary A.

We often think of you John & Diana

Wishing you every happiness in your new home.
Daphne and Graham

all good wishes, Sylvia & John

We shall miss you - with much love Joan R.

God bless you Ralph
& Thank you for everything.
& Pip

Wishing you both good health &
lots of happiness in Hungerford.
Much love. Pat